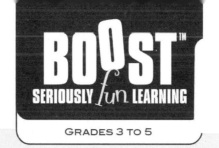

Story of the Vikings Coloring Book

by A. G. Smith

DOVER PUBLICATIONS, INC., Mineola, New York

For Joan Magee

Bibliographical Note

BOOST Story of the Vikings Coloring Book, first published by Dover Publications, Inc., in 2013, is a revised edition of *Story of the Vikings Coloring Book,* originally published by Dover in 1988..

International Standard Book Number

ISBN-13: 978-0-486-49439-5
ISBN-10: 0-486-49439-X

Manufactured in the United States by Courier Corporation
49439X01   2013
www.doverpublications.com

Introduction

One of the most colorful periods in history was the Viking Age (roughly 800-1100 A.D.), when the Scandinavian peoples entered the international scene in an unparalleled burst of activity—often violent. During this period, the nations of Denmark, Norway, and Sweden were molded out of small chieftaincies and principalities, and became Christian realms. Iceland, Greenland, and a section of North America were colonized by Norsemen, who also raided and settled in parts of the British Isles and northwestern mainland Europe. Viking traders and dynasts loomed large on Russian soil. Scandinavian mercenaries served the Byzantine emperors; Scandinavian merchants trafficked with the caliphs of Baghdad.

To the Christianized, sedentary Frankish, Anglo-Saxon, and Irish chroniclers, the first Vikings seemed to be murderous demons who had appeared out of nowhere, and this is the romantic reputation that they have retained in the popular memory. Actually, the Scandinavians, northernmost and most remote of the Germanic peoples, were merely still in a phase of historical development that the other Germanic groups, and continental Celts, has already passed through and largely forgotten: the Heroic Age. A multitude of mutually hostile local warlords—with retinues of fighting men personally loyal to them, and with court bards to praise their valor and curse their enemies—ruled over a much larger population of farmers and herdsmen (with some mixture of slaves, either purchased or captured in combat).

The Scandinavian region was already fairly prosperous in late Roman times, thanks to its iron ore and furs, and enjoyed far-flung trade relations, as archaeological excavations have shown. (For the whole history of Scandinavia through Viking times, archaeology has proved to be a more reliable source of knowledge than either the unsympathetic and incomplete reports made by the Vikings' victims and enemies, or even than the Old Norse sagas, which were written centuries after the events they chronicle and freely mix fantasy with fact). The early "dark ages," characterized by wholesale migrations of populations, were disruptive in Scandinavia as elsewhere, but international trade continued and beautiful works of art were created (see the helmet on page 33). By about 800, various social and economic pressures at home combined with favorable outward circumstances to bring about the great Viking explosion whose political, technological, and artistic results are recorded in the pictures and captions of the *Story of the Vikings Coloring Book.*

Although this book follows the common practice of using the term *Vikings* loosely as a synonym of the Scandinavians or Norsemen of the period, actually it should strictly be applied only to those individuals who set out on raiding expeditions in quest of plunder and adventure, temporarily leaving behind them their regular employment as farmers and the like. The etymology of *Viking* is disputed, like so much else pertaining to these people. The information in the present book makes use of the most recent generally shared opinions of recognized experts in the field. After a view of the Norse homeland (page 5), the Vikings' ships—chief instruments of their success as raiders and traders—are pictured and described on pages 6 through 13. Pages 14 through 32 provide a survey of the military and political history of the age, including a number of famous voyages, battles, and other events. The last part of the book, pages 33 through 48, is devoted to the everyday life and the arts and crafts of the Vikings: weaponry, metalwork, carving on wood and stone, religion, runes, literature, and other aspects of this fascinating era.

The homelands of the Norsemen, or Vikings, were in Scandinavia and on the islands of the Baltic Sea. Scandinavia is a region made up of the present-day countries of Denmark, Norway, and Sweden. As in this Norwegian scene, the land available for growing crops was often just a narrow strip on the shores of fjords. A fjord is a long, narrow bay of the sea between cliffs.

Historians have suggested many reasons for the overseas expansion that ushered in the Viking Age about 800 A.D. Overpopulation and limited opportunities at home may have been causes. Some experts believe that a warming climate may have led to the expansion. With less sea ice in the fjords, the Vikings could sail more often.

RI.3.1 Ask and answer questions to demonstrate understanding of a text, referring explicitly to the text as the basis for the answers. Also **RI.3.2, RI.3.3, RI.3.7, L.3.4.d; RI.4.1, RI.4.2, RI.4.3, RI.4.8, L.4.4.c; RI.5.1, RI.5.2, RI.5.8, L.5.4.c.**

5

The Vikings' ships made their expansion possible. As shipbuilders they were unsurpassed at the time. Over centuries they developed ships with true keels and with hulls of lapstrake (or clinker) construction—overlapping planks riveted together. This building method helped Vikings make ships that were strong and flexible. The shallow draft of these ships enabled them to land on almost any beach. They could also sail far up inlets and rivers, allowing startling surprise attacks.

 RI.3.2 Determine the main idea of a text; recount the key details and explain how they support the main idea. Also **RI.3.3, RI.3.4, RI.3.8; RI.4.2, RI.4.3, RI.4.4, RI.4.8; RI.5.2, RI.5.3, RI.5.4, RI.5.8.**

Viking ships were relatively light. This made it possible for them to be portaged,
or hauled overland, around rapids or between bodies of water. This scene shows Vikings
transporting their ship in Russia in the ninth century.

 RI.3.4 Determine the meaning of general academic and domain-specific words and phrases
in a text relevant to a *grade 3 topic or subject area*. Also **RI.3.2, RI.3.7, RI.3.10; RI.4.2,
RI.4.4, RI.4.10; RI.5.4, RI.5.10.**

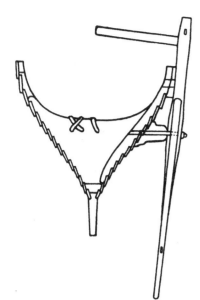

THE VIKING SHIP

The ship shown here is based on a 76-foot-long ship from the mid-ninth century. It was discovered in 1880 at Gokstad, Norway, and is now in the Viking Ship Museum in Oslo.

Steering Board

Viking ships were steered by a rudder. It was located on the right side of the ship rather than at the stern. The rudder was attached by a rope or strip. The term *starboard* ("steering side") for the right side of a ship is derived from this setup.

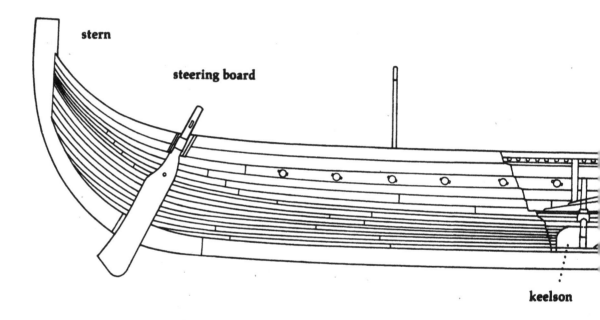

stern

steering board

keelson

oar-hole cover

rigging block

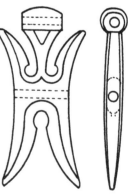

Lapstrake (or Clinker) Construction

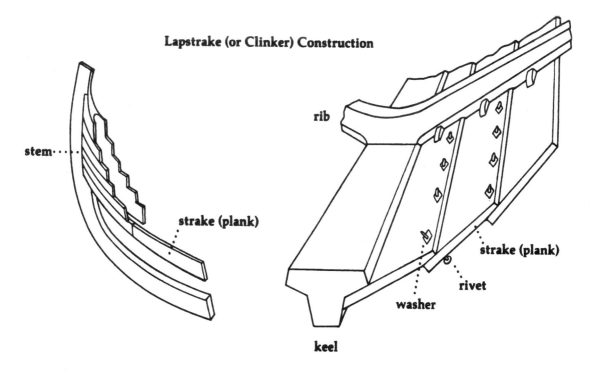

stem

strake (plank)

rib

strake (plank)

rivet

washer

keel

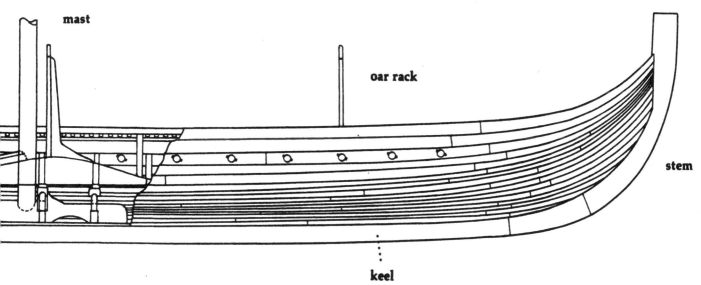

mast

oar rack

stem

keel

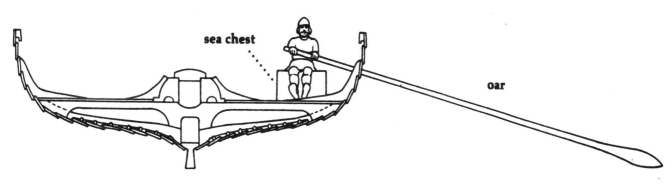

sea chest

oar

Frame System

Various types of Viking ships are known from literary sources and from actual discoveries. Shown here is a ship more or less like the ones discovered at Gokstad and Oseberg, Norway. It has oars for moving near shore or on rivers as well as large square sails for use at sea. The Oseberg ship was built in about 800 and discovered in 1903. It too can be found in the Viking Ship Museum in Oslo. Unlike the Gokstad ship, the Oseberg ship had a shield rack like the one illustrated here.

 RI.3.2 Determine the main idea of a text; recount the key details and explain how they support the main idea. Also **RI.3.1, RI.3.7; RI.4.1, RI.4.2, RI.4.3, RI.4.7; RI.5.1, RI.5.3.**

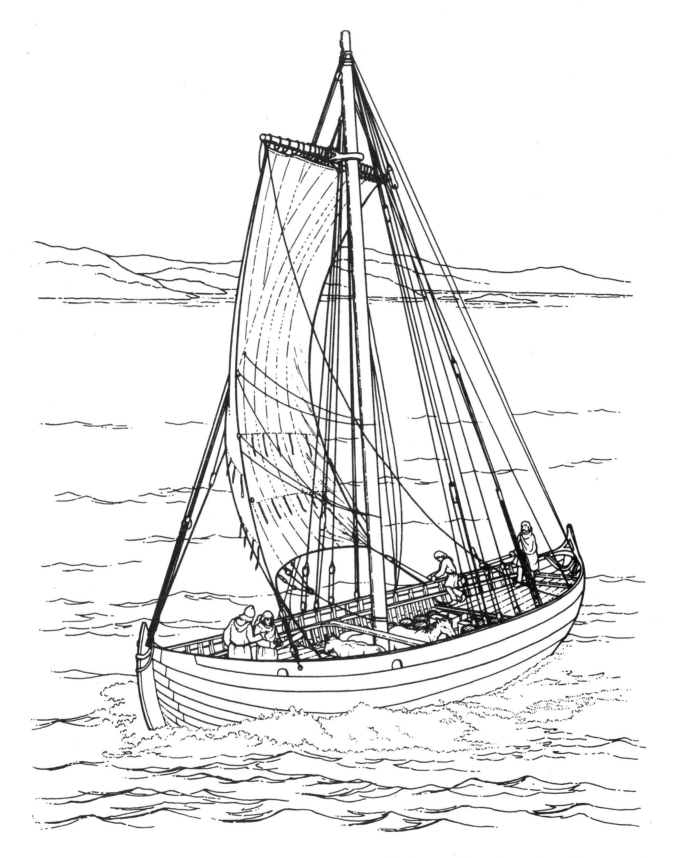

The shallow-draft ships so far described were used by coastal raiders. These ships are often all classified together as longships. But some were much longer than the Gokstad ship. For settlement, trade, and exploration on the high seas, more seaworthy types (like the ones shown here and on the next page) were used. They were shorter and of deeper draft. They also had much more room for cargo.

The Vikings were fearless sailors. They even braved the sometimes dangerous North Atlantic in open ships. It has been said that the Vikings' true home was the sea.

RI.3.1 Ask and answer questions to demonstrate understanding of a text, referring explicitly to the text as the basis for the answers. Also **RI.3.6, SL.3.1a; RI.4.1, RI.4.8, SL.4.1.a; RI.5.1, RI.5.8, SL.5.1.a.**

Viking navigators did not possess compasses. They calculated their position on the open sea using the sun or the stars. They were also aided by a bearing dial and a stick with the sun's posi-tion marked at significant latitudes. The Vikings also took sound-ings, measuring off the line by their arm span. The term *fathom* for this six-foot length is derived from the Norse word for it.

RI.3.3 Describe the relationship between a series of historical events, scientific ideas or concepts, or steps in technical procedures in a text, using language that pertains to time, sequence, and cause/effect. Also **RI.3.4, L.3.4.d; RI.4.3, RI.4.4, L.4.4.c; RI.5.3, RI.5.4, L.5.4.c.**

 RI.3.1 Ask and answer questions to demonstrate understanding of a text, referring explicitly to the text as the basis for the answers. Also **RI.3.2, RI.3.3, RI.3.7; RI.4.1, RI.4.2, RI.4.3, RI.4.5, RI.4.7; RI.5.1, RI.5.2, RI.5.3.**

There had been Viking activity on English coasts before 793. However, a raid for plunder on the monastery island of Lindisfarne (now called Holy Island) off the Northumbrian coast that year awakened the European West to the significance of the Viking presence. Raids on northern England, Scotland, and Ireland continued into the ninth century. These early attacks were pirate raids carried out by lesser chieftains. As the joining of forces and the beginnings of national states progressed in Denmark, Norway, and Sweden, regular armies left Scandinavia for the British Isles. Raiding gave way to military occupation and civilian settlement.

By 851 the Vikings were occupying parts of England. Their success there was helped by the division of the territory among the rival dynasties of Wessex, Mercia, East Anglia, and Northumbria. After severe setbacks, Alfred the Great of Wessex, the southernmost kingdom, defeated the Vikings at Edington in 878. The victory saved the south for the Anglo-Saxons. By the ensuing treaty (shown above) the Viking army leader Guthrum withdrew to East Anglia, thus rounding out the already partly formed Danelaw, as the Vikings' large portion of England came to be known.

 RI.3.4 Determine the meaning of general academic and domain-specific words and phrases in a text relevant to a *grade 3 topic or subject area.* Also **RI.3.2, RI.3.3, RF.3.4.a; RI.4.2, RI.4.4, RF.4.4.a; RI.5.2, RI.5.4, RF.5.4.a.**

The Vikings were colonists as well as warriors. As early as the end of the eighth century they were already settling in the Orkney, Shetland, and Hebrides Islands off the coasts of Scotland. Livestock raising and fishing were the main livelihoods. The illustration shows the stone and turf farm buildings of Jarlshof in the Shetlands. The Norse-style name means "earl's house." It comes from a novel by Sir Walter Scott, though the site had been in use since the Bronze Age.

 RI.3.7 Use information gained from illustrations and the words in a text to demonstrate understanding of the text. Also **RI.3.2, RI.3.3, RI.3.10; RI.4.2, RI.4.3, RI.4.5, RI.4.7, RI.4.10; RI.5.3, RI.5.10.**

By the end of the ninth century the Vikings had colonized the Faroe Islands. They were settling in Iceland by about 860. That island had scarcely been populated earlier. Soon, it was full of successful farms with sod-built houses. The illustration shows such a farmhouse at Stöng, where a modern reconstruction exists. During the same century the Vikings were also settling in Ireland and at York in northern England.

RI.3.1 Ask and answer questions to demonstrate understanding of a text, referring explicitly to the text as the basis for the answers. Also **RI.3.2, RI.3.3, SL.3.1; RI.4.1, RI.4.2, RI.4.3, SL.4.1; RI.5.1, RI.5.2, RI.5.3, SL.5.1.**

In 930 Iceland became a republic. The chief political institution was the annual Althing ("general assembly"). At this gathering, 36 of the leading islanders met to establish laws and settle disputes. They met in an encampment at Thingvellir, a rocky ridge at the edge of a grassy plain in southwestern Iceland. *Thingvellir* means "Assembly Plain" or "Parliament Plain." This drawing shows a "lawspeaker" holding forth at the foot of Law Rock. It is based on an 1873 painting by the English artist W. G. Collingwood. Iceland lost its independence to Norway in 1262.

 RI.3.1 Ask and answer questions to demonstrate understanding of a text, referring explicitly to the text as the basis for the answers. Also **RI.3.2, RI.3.3, RI.3.7; RI.4.1, RI.4.2, RI.4.3, RI.4.7; RI.5.1, RI.5.2, RI.5.3.**

Viking raids on France began in the 840s. Eventually Norse armies wintered in France, as they did in England. The most striking event in France was the unsuccessful Viking takeover of Paris in 885 (shown in the illustration). The greatest Norse success came in 911. That year, the Viking chieftain Rollo (Hrolf) was made the first Duke of Normandy by the Carolingian king Charles the Simple. Rollo was given the title in exchange for his allegiance and his help in expelling other Vikings. This was the beginning of the amazing rise and worldwide expansion of the Normans.

The people called Rus in early Russian chronicles were possibly of mixed origin. But they certainly included Swedish Viking traders. The city of Novgorod is shown here. It was traditionally founded in about 860 by the Rus chieftain Rurick. He supposedly is also the ancestor of the great dynasty that came to rule farther south in Kiev. In 839 the Rus sent ambassadors to the court of the Byzantine emperor. By the 860s they had begun attacking his capital, Constantinople. Viking trade in eastern Europe was extensive. Islamic goods and coins flowed into Scandinavia from southwestern and central Asia.

About 985, Eric (Eirik) the Red, who had been outlawed from both Norway and Iceland, discovered Greenland. He founded a colony there on the south coast. About fifteen years later, his son Leif followed up a chance sighting of new lands to the southwest with a planned exploration. Settlement followed later. Controversy rages over exactly which areas of North America the Vikings knew as Vinland (almost surely meaning "grape country"), Markland ("forest country") and other names. Certainly L'Anse aux Meadows on Newfoundland is a true Viking site. This drawing is based on an 1893 painting by the Norwegian artist Christian Krohg depicting the Viking discovery of America.

The Vikings called the native people of North America Skraelings. Their first encounters were friendly. The Norsemen traded woven cloth and other goods for furs. Conflict developed, however. After a few years the Greenlanders were forced to abandon their settlements.

 RI.3.1 Ask and answer questions to demonstrate understanding of a text, referring explicitly to the text as the basis for the answers. Also **RI.3.2, RI.3.3, SL.3.1.d; RI.4.1, RI.4.2, RI.4.3, SL.4.1.d; RI.5.1, RI.5.2, SL.5.1.d.**

Another term for Norsemen in eastern Europe was Varangians. From about the year 1000 on, some Norsemen were employed by Byzantine emperors. They served as bodyguards—the famous Varangian Guard, of which Harald Hardråde (later king of Norway and invader of England) was a member. The Vikings reached Athens, too. A large marble lion was found in the harbor of Piraeus. It bears carved runic markings on its shoulder. The statue is now at the entrance to the Arsenal in Venice.

 RI.3.2 Determine the main idea of a text; recount the key details and explain how they support the main idea. Also **RI.3.3, RI.3.10; RI.4.2, RI.4.3, RI.4.10; RI.5.2, RI.5.3, RI.5.10.**

During the Viking period, Denmark, Norway, and Sweden were steadily becoming unified nations under powerful rulers. The process had frequent conflicts. In or about the year 1000 the Norwegian king Olaf Tryggvason was killed in the sea battle of Svolder (Swold) in the Baltic. He was defeated by a group of Swedes under their king Olaf Skötkonung and the Danes under the forceful Svein (Sweyn) Forkbeard. During sea fighting, masts were taken down. Ships were often fastened together like floating fortresses.

 RI.3.1 Ask and answer questions to demonstrate understanding of a text, referring explicitly to the text as the basis for the answers. Also **RI.3.2, RI.3.4, RF.3.4.a; RI.4.1, RI.4.2, RI.4.4, RF.4.4.a; RI.5.1, RI.5.2, RI.5.4, RF.5.4.a.**

Svein Forkbeard, the Danish king, was also successful in England. Anglo-Saxon kings paid the Norsemen huge sums of money and goods in tribute, known as Danegeld. Tribute is money paid from one nation to another in exchange for peace. Invasions still continued. Finally in 1013 Svein conquered the south of England. The drawing shows a Viking attack on a fortified Anglo-Saxon *tun* (town). Denmark and England were then joined into one kingdom until 1042. The most famous ruler in this period was Svein's son Canute (Knut).

 CCSS **RI.3.2** Determine the main idea of a text; recount the key details and explain how they support the main idea. Also **RI.3.3, RI.3.7, L.3.4.a; RI.4.2, RI.4.3, RI.4.7, L.4.4.a; RI.5.2, RI.5.3, L.5.4.a.**

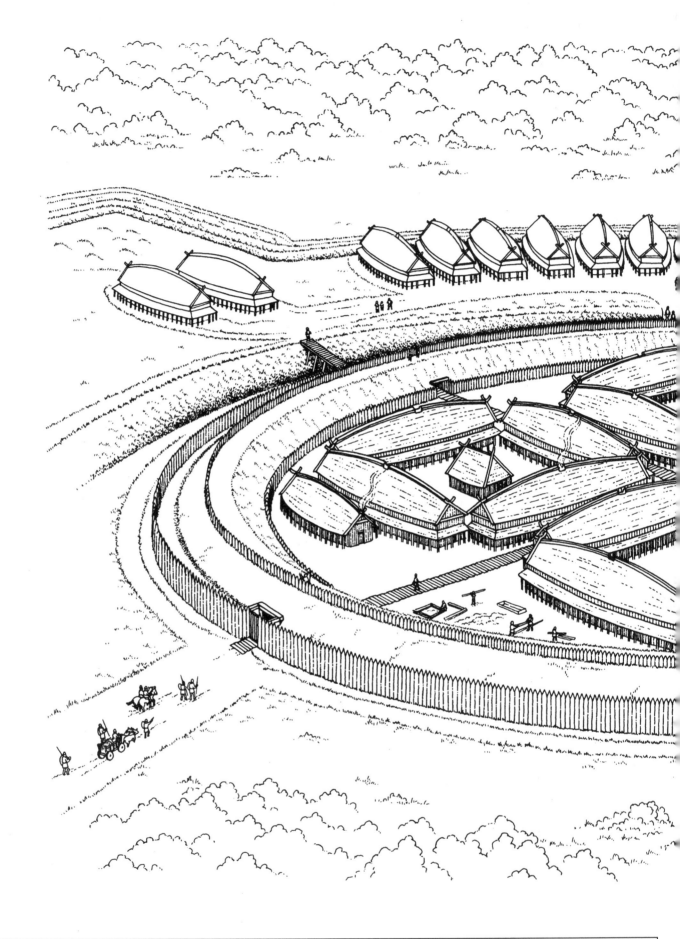

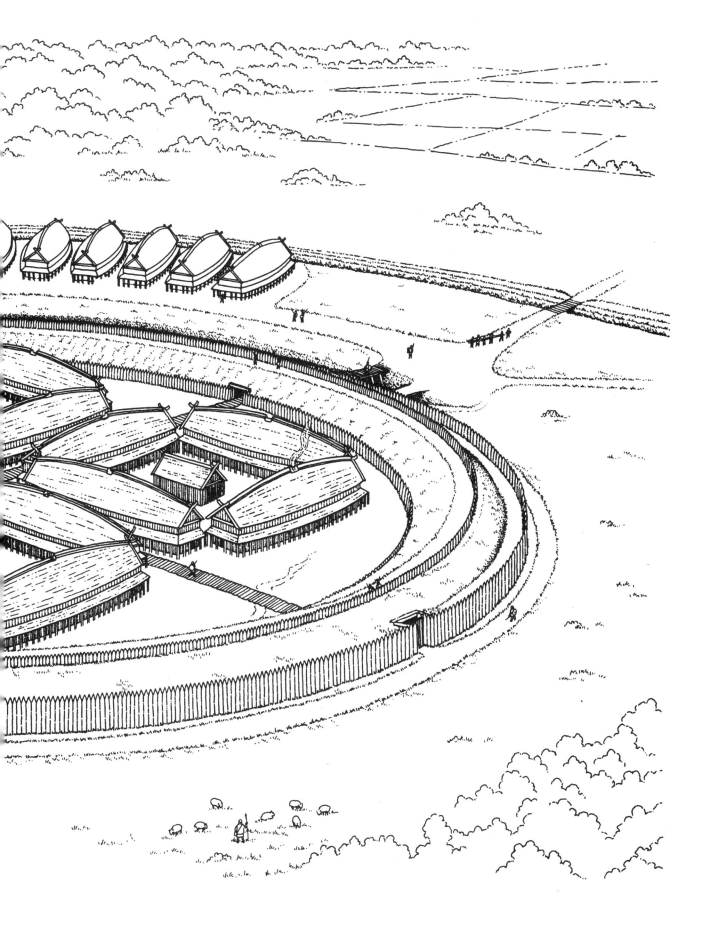

Svein, Canute, and even earlier Danish kings knew it was important to maintain control in Denmark while they pursued their adventures abroad. They set up a system of fortified camps. The camps had military posts of up to 1,200 men each.

These regional strongholds had earthen walls strengthened by fences made of pointed stakes. Illustrated is the camp at Trelleborg. The boat-shaped buildings in the background served as housing for soldiers.

31

The last major Viking adventure in England was the Norwegian king Harald Hardraade's invasion in 1066. It is seen by some historians as the effective end of the Viking Age. Harald tried to claim the throne. The new Anglo-Saxon king Harold Godwinsson defeated Harald at Stamford Bridge in Yorkshire on September 25 (see illustration). However, King Harold was overpowered by the Normans, led by William the Conqueror, at Hastings on the south coast nineteen days later.

  RI.3.1 Ask and answer questions to demonstrate understanding of a text, referring explicitly to the text as the basis for the answers. Also **RI.3.3, RI.3.10; RI.4.1, RI.4.3, RI.4.10; RI.5.1, RI.5.3, RI.5.10.**

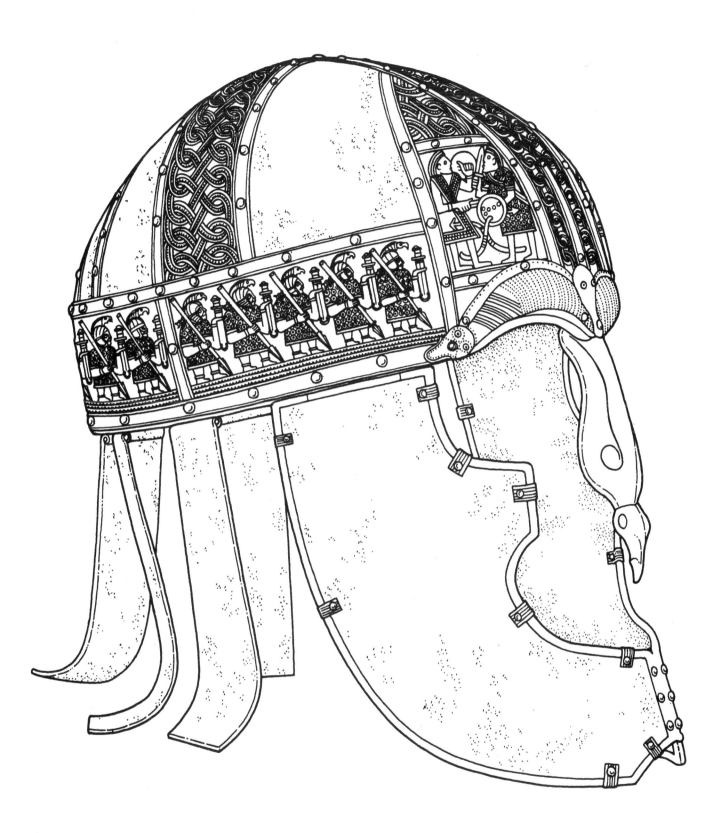

The arts, crafts, and daily life of the Vikings had developed gradually over several centuries. One of the finest objects preserved from immediately pre-Viking times is this magnificent bronze-ornamented iron helmet. It is from the Vendel culture in the Uppland region of Sweden. The life and civilization of the pre-Viking era in Sweden are clearly reflected in the Old English epic poem *Beowulf*. This work was composed in the eighth century.

Viking home life centered around the hearth in a long hall. Benches along the sides served as beds for most of the household. Smoke escaped through a small vent in the roof.

Storytelling (seen here) was a favorite entertainment. In royal and noble homes, feasting was often spectacular.

Woolen cloth was the most important textile made by the Vikings. It was woven on standing looms. The warp threads were kept straight by stone or clay weights. The woman in this picture is beating the thread into place with a wooden "weaving sword." Viking women not only directed household affairs. They had much more independence as property owners and greater power in divorce procedures than other European women of the time.

 RI.3.7 Use information gained from illustrations and the words in a text to demonstrate understanding of the text. Also **RI.3.2, RI.3.3; RI.4.2, RI.4.3, RI.4.7; RI.5.2, RI.5.3.**

The armorer, or weaponsmith, forged swords, battleaxes, and spears. He also made helmets, chain mail, and shields for defense. Chain mail is a kind of flexible armor.

 RI.3.4 Determine the meaning of general academic and domain-specific words and phrases in a text relevant to a *grade 3 topic or subject area.* Also **RI.3.1, RI.3.2, L.3.4.d; RI.4.1, RI.4.2, L.4.4.c; RI.5.1, RI.5.2, L.5.4.c.**

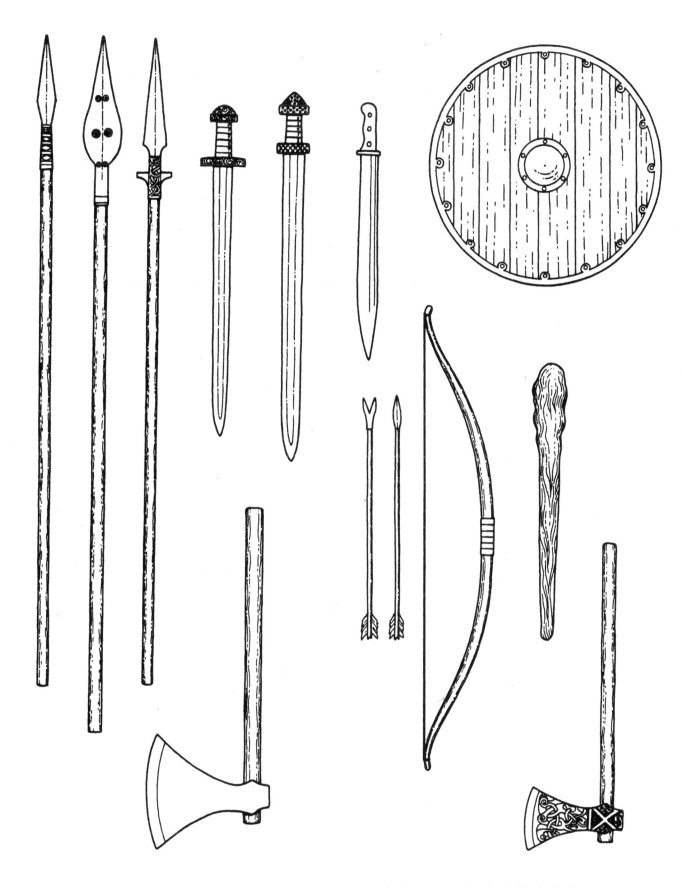

Viking weapons were often decorated with inlays of silver wire and niello (a black alloy).
The shields were brightly painted.

 RI.3.7 Use information gained from illustrations and the words in a text to demonstrate understanding of the text. Also **RI.3.1, RI.3.4, L.3.6; RI.4.1, RI.4.4, RI.4.7, L.4.6; RI.5.1, RI.5.4, L.5.6.**

The Vikings were excellent horsemen. A warrior's horse was sometimes buried with him. Only a wealthy chieftain like the one pictured could afford a shirt of chain mail. Stirrups were invented in the Far East about 200 B.C. They reached Europe in the eighth century A.D. and were known in Viking Scandinavia. The Normans, of Viking origin, made use of their soldiers on horseback in their conquest of England in 1066.

Personal disputes between Norsemen were often settled by combat. This sometimes took the form of a duel on a small island. This duel was called a *holmganga* ("island-going").

Killings often escalated into long-running feuds between families. A system was devised by which survivors could be compensated financially for the loss of kinsmen.

 RI.3.2 Determine the main idea of a text; recount the key details and explain how they support the main idea. Also **RI.3.3, RI.3.10, L.3.4.d; RI.4.2, RI.4.3, RI.4.10, L.4.4.c; RI.5.3, RI.5.10, L.5.4.c.**

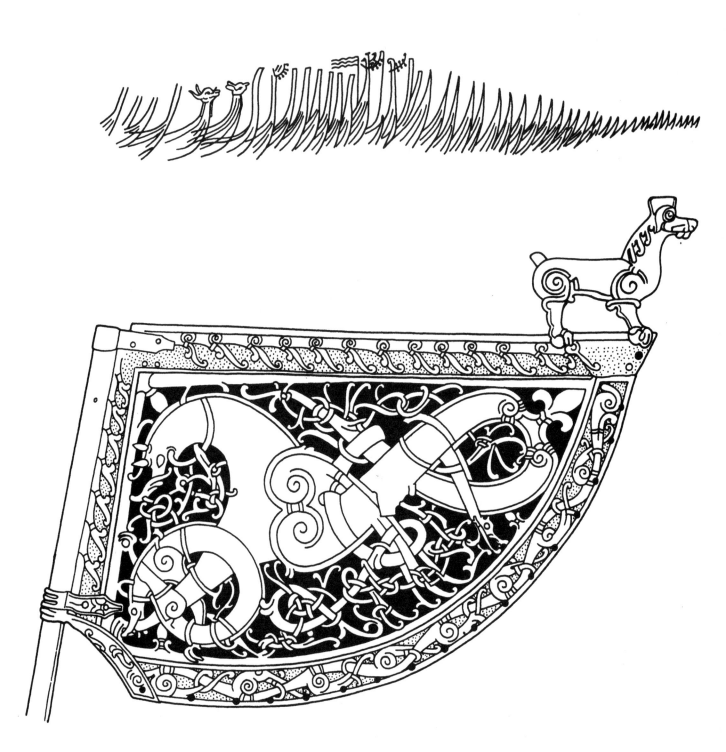

Ships were the most prized possessions of the Vikings. They often had colorful names, such as *Long Dragon, Crane,* and *Long Serpent.* Ships sometimes had detailed decorations. The upper drawing shows a Viking fleet with ornamented prows. It is based on a wood carving excavated at Bergen, Norway. Below that is a gilt-bronze weather vane that decorated either the masthead or the prow of a longship. It represents a "great beast." The vane probably dates from the eleventh century.

 RI.3.4 Determine the meaning of general academic and domain-specific words and phrases in a text relevant to a *grade 3 topic or subject area.* Also **RI.3.1, RI.3.2, RI.3.7; RI.4.1, RI.4.2, RI.4.7; RI.5.1, RI.5.2.**

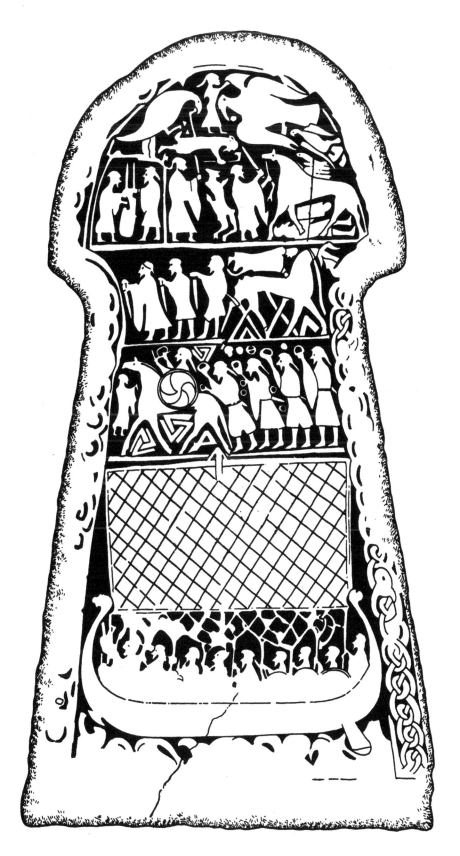

The drawing shows a picture stone from the Swedish island of Gotland. It dates back to the eighth century. This limestone shaft was originally about eleven feet high. Some two feet of it are now missing. The top level depicts a battle. The next level probably shows a burial. The scene below that likely represents fallen Vikings entering Valhalla. This was believed to be the special afterlife abode of heroes. At the bottom is a warship. Such stones were often set up as memorials of people or events.

RI.3.7 Use information gained from illustrations and the words in a text to demonstrate understanding of the text. Also **RI.3.1, RI.3.2, RF.3.4.a, SL.3.1; RI.4.1, RI.4.2, RI.4.7, SL.4.1; RI.5.1, RI.5.2, SL.5.1.**

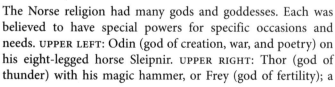

The Norse religion had many gods and goddesses. Each was believed to have special powers for specific occasions and needs. UPPER LEFT: Odin (god of creation, war, and poetry) on his eight-legged horse Sleipnir. UPPER RIGHT: Thor (god of thunder) with his magic hammer, or Frey (god of fertility); a three-inch-high bronze statuette. LOWER LEFT: Bronze statuette of Frey from Rällinge, Sweden. LOWER RIGHT: Pendant depicting a woman with a drinking horn. She is possibly a celestial warrior maiden called a Valkyrie welcoming a fallen hero to Valhalla.

 RI.3.1 Ask and answer questions to demonstrate understanding of a text, referring explicitly to the text as the basis for the answers. Also **RI.3.2, RI.3.4, L.3.6; RI.4.1, RI.4.2, RI.4.4, L.4.6; RI.5.1, RI.5.4, L.5.6.**

f u th a r n i s t b z l R

A granite block with runic inscriptions is pictured here. It is from the Södermanland province of Sweden. The stone is five feet, three inches high. Runes were letter forms used at the time in many areas of Europe for writing the local language. Such languages included Norse and Old English. Their angular form was suited to their original use: incisions on wood. The thirteen-sign alphabet shown is the simplified but imperfect one used in Denmark in the Viking age. The equivalent in our alphabet appears below each sign (*th* is pronounced as in *thin*; *R* stands for a special *r*-sound).

 RI.3.7 Use information gained from illustrations and the words in a text to demonstrate understanding of the text. Also **RI.3.1, RI.3.3, RI.3.4, RI.3.10; RI.4.1, RI.4.3, RI.4.4, RI.4.10; RI.5.1, RI.5.3, RI.5.4, RI.5.10.**

Court poetry was composed in many Viking lands. Another **major** form of literature was the prose sagas. They were mostly **royal,** local, or family histories written mainly in Iceland from **the** eleventh through the fourteenth centuries. In the foreground **above** is Snorri Sturluson (1179–1241). He is considered by many to be the greatest saga writer. In the background is the climactic scene from *Njal's Saga*. This saga from about the year 1280 is about a widespread family feud. The illustration shows the burning of Njal's home, with the family inside. This work is often thought of as the finest single saga. The author is unknown.

 RI.3.2 Determine the main idea of a text; recount the key details and explain how they support the main idea. Also **RI.3.1, RI.3.4, RI.3.7; RI.4.1, RI.4.2, RI.4.4, RI.4.7; RI.5.1, RI.5.2, RI.5.4.**

Another excellent saga is *Egil's Saga* from about the year 1230. It may have been written by Snorri. Its hero, Egil Skallagrimsson, was a major poet and a ruthless fighting man. He lived from about 910 to 990. The illustration shows the scene from the saga in which Egil carries the body of his drowned son Bodvar to the family burial mound. Later, Egil composed his finest poem, "Lament for My Sons." It is included in the saga.

 RI.3.1 Ask and answer questions to demonstrate understanding of a text, referring explicitly to the text as the basis for the answers. Also **RI.3.2, RI.3.7, RI.3.10; RI.4.1, RI.4.2, RI.4.7, RI.4.10; RI.5.1, RI.5.10.**

Christianity spread in the Scandinavian countries during the tenth and eleventh centuries. The twelfth and thirteenth centuries in Norway saw the construction of many churches. These buildings were much more elaborate than most Viking architecture had been. Illustrated is the church at Borgund (ca. 1200). The dragon heads on the gables hark back to pagan days.

RI.3.2 Determine the main idea of a text; recount the key details and explain how they support the main idea. Also **RI.3.3, RI.3.7, SL.3.1.a; RI.4.2, RI.4.3, RI.4.7, SL.4.1.a; RI.5.2, RI.5.3, SL.5.1.a.**

This is the doorway of another Norwegian church. It is richly carved with interlacing animal and floral designs. Birds, snakes, and dragons intertwine their necks, bodies, and legs in fantastic patterns. These patterns were inspired by earlier Viking art.

 RI.3.1 Ask and answer questions to demonstrate understanding of a text, referring explicitly to the text as the basis for the answers. Also **RI.3.2, RI.3.7; RI.4.1, RI.4.2, RI.4.7; RI.5.1.**

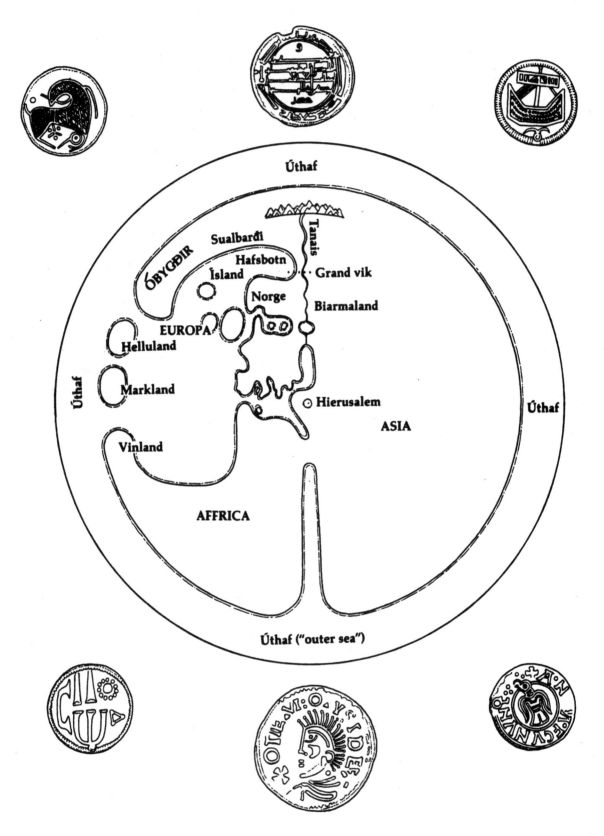

As the map in the center shows, the Vikings thought of the world as one large landmass and several islands in a great endless sea. Also illustrated are a few of the types of coins found in Viking graves. At the top left is an early coin minted at Hedeby, Denmark. It is from between the years 800 and 825. Next to it is an Islamic coin acquired through commerce. At the bottom right is a silver penny showing a raven. It dates back to roughly the year 940 and is from the Viking kingdom of York, England.